Lady

Always Remember God has a plan! (Jeremiah 29:11)

DEVASTATED
BUT
Not Destroyed

DEVASTATED
BUT
Not Destroyed

Jessica L. Jones

DMI PUBLISHING HOUSE
WINSTON-SALEM

DEVASTATED BUT NOT DESTROYED
Copyright © 2014 - Jessica L. Jones

Take note that the name satan and related names are not capitalized. We choose not to acknowledge him, even to the point of violating grammatical rules.

Cover Design: Tia W. Cooke

Library of Congress Control Number: 2014959786
ISBN 978-0-692-34201-5

DMI Publishing House
(a division of Dominion Media International, LLC)
3733 Ogburn Avenue
Winston-Salem, VA 23487
www.dominionmediainternational.com

This book and all DMI Publishing House books are available at Christian bookstores and distributors worldwide.

Printed in the United States of America. - First Edition

Dedication

Father, my ultimate desire is that You be glorified in my life. Through every fault, failure, and fall, You still saw purpose and destiny in me. I am humbled by and grateful for Your grace. May the world know my love for You and Your unconditional love for them. I love You! Matthew 5:16 – the glory is Yours!

In memory of my loving mother Loretta R. Jones – your dream is my reality.

To my 'Daddy' Sherman Jones, Sr. – You believed in me and always said to me, "You're going to put Brodnax, Virginia on the map." I am thankful that God chose you to be my Daddy. I love you! 'Ma' Rebecca Jones – Thanks for listening to the rough draft and I finished first (smile). Love you! Angela and Sherman Jr. – You're next! Amaze the world with all God has placed within you!

Angela Collins – Mama, you are a jewel! Thanks for believing, listening, and always being there. Every prayer and every push has made me better and I am grateful for you I love you. Uncle James and Aunt Joyce - Thank you for your support. You mean the world to me! Chanel Wright – You are a blessing! May the Lord reward you for your kindness. Love you!

Pastor Ron and Pastor Patrice Thornhill – One word from the prophet can change the course of your life. You heard from God, spoke what He said, and look what the Lord has done! I thank God for you and I thank you for obeying God. I love both of you!

My family, Tabernacle of Zion Church Family, Pastor Vanessa, Elder Ivan, Nzingha, April, Jasmine, Sharleda, Tanequa, and EVERYONE that genuinely prayed, supported and believed – Thank you and I love you!

To the hands that hold this book you will find
strength,

To the eyes that read these pages you will find hope,

To the heart that has become weary you will find
help,

And to the warrior that has been wounded you will
learn that although it was intended to be fatal, it was
not final and you will find a reason to fight again.

Although you were devastated,
you were not destroyed!

Table of Contents

Foreword

One of the most challenging issues confronting the body of Christ and the world at large is learning how to bounce back from life's storms. While some know the feeling of devastation, others have had to battle with self-destruction. However, regardless of whether you have felt disenfranchised, discouraged, or even on the brink of feeling destroyed, this book provides hope. Moreover, with the difficulties confronting our nation, there is a clarion call for healing. Pastor Jessica does a masterful job in prescribing the ultimate medicine, "Devastated But Not Destroyed." This book is a must read for those of us who walk daily through our own valleys and know the gut wrenching feeling of being in the shadows of death yet to be reminded that the Lord is still with us.

Ronald Thornhill, M. Div.
Senior Pastor, Tabernacle of Zion Church

Life Happens

Life happens. Unexpectedly, without warning, and often times without your permission, everything can change in a moment. In spite of how well you plan, there are some variables in life for which you cannot prepare. No one wakes up and anticipates being diagnosed with a terminal illness. No one goes to work expecting to be terminated. No one looks for a phone call that their loved one has tragically lost their life. Everyone lives, but no one plans for life to happen to them.

Life happens. Without warning, all that was once peaceful can immediately be painful. All that was once normal, in an instant becomes unfamiliar. If you are not careful, the pain of a "moment" can paralyze and render you emotionally incapacitated. There are people today (perhaps even you) who are held hostage by what has happened in life. Although the pain of the experience is over, the residue of hurt has hindered them from moving forward. That is the purpose of this book. It is my prayer that this book will serve as a manual of instruction and encouragement to help you move forward during challenging times. I know all too well how it feels to be gripped by unexpected tragedy, but also how to survive and thrive against the odds. It is my hope that you will find strength and comfort as you navigate through these pages and make peace with this liberating truth: although it was devastating, it did not destroy you.

Merriam Webster Dictionary defines **devastate** as *to destroy much or most of (something): to cause great* *damage or harm to (something), to cause (someone) to feel extreme emotional pain.* Dealing with something that is devastating is never easy. I can recall while I was a teenager, my mother was diagnosed with cancer and we learned that it was terminal. I was devastated. I was too young to express my fears, concerns, and even questions, but I knew that I hurt because she was hurting. No amount of conversations with my daddy, relatives, or hospice workers prepared me for the news of her departure on that Christmas day around 5:00 pm. I was the definition of devastated, but I had a choice and ultimately we all do when life happens. I could choose to die in the pain of that moment – surely the pain was great – and become emotionally incapacitated or I could choose to live through it and process the pain properly.

You see, Mama was an exceptional woman and she taught me what faith looked like in the midst of her fight. She constantly reminded me, our family, and friends of her favorite scripture which was Proverbs 3:5-6 which says,

"Trust in the LORD with all thine heart; and lean not unto thine own understanding. In all thy ways acknowledge him, and he shall direct thy paths."

My mama was allowing faith to do what it does best and that is to trust God even when you are not able to trace what He is doing. She taught me that tears are not always a sign of doubt or defeat but sometimes they water the seeds of faith that have grown weary. Though I was battling devastation, my mama had found peace and had a relentless faith that trusted God because she was living to live again.

Devastation can make you feel like you are dying. It can put you in a position where you have to choose whether you will simply exist – too hurt to love, live, laugh, or move forward – or rather LIVE while allowing the pain to serve as a reminder that you survived. I chose to live. I can remember sitting at my godmother's piano after my mother's memorial service and in the stillness of that moment, I was filled with anger, resentment, questions – you name it, I believe I had it. Then I heard a still, small voice in the depth of my soul whisper, "*I'll never leave you nor will I forsake you and I'll hold you until you can stand again.*" In that moment, divine assistance had come. Although the help was there, I had to choose to align myself with life.

You cannot afford to simply exist; you have to choose to live. When the storms of life come and leave you so devastated that all you can see is destruction, you have to choose to live. Life is not easy in the midst of adversity or in the face of controversy; but, there is a sufficient grace available in God to strengthen you when you are weak. There is a peace available in God that will surpass your understanding and hold your mind together when your world is falling apart. Life happens, but God is faithful and more than capable to provide all that you need.

Master the Moment

Moments are an important part of how you handle devastation. Moments determine whether or not you will face devastation with denial or head on, giving yourself the time and space to properly process what you are facing. A friend of mine and I were talking one day about the demands of ministry, and the common stressors of everyday life. I jokingly said, "Sometimes, you just need to take a minute for your moment." After stating that, something resonated within me. You and I need to learn the art of *taking a minute to work through the moment.*

We all have moments in life. Even as you reflect now, there have been moments that have caused you to smile and brought you great joy; yet others have caused you to cry while enduring great pain. Moments will happen to all of us. It does not matter how educated you are, how successful you are, or how young you are. There will come a time when you will face a situation that is beyond your control. Ultimately, if you do not learn how to master the moments in your life, they will master you!

Moments are temporary. They are not designed to last long, but often the situations that occur in the moments of our lives can make them feel like forever. I would like to provide you with a new definition of "a moment." A *moment* is any point or time where the enemy attempts to suffocate God's promise concerning you with the circumstances you are presently encountering. When you are able to recognize the strategy of the enemy and also realize you already have the victory, you will be unstoppable. Part of the enemy's strategy is to make you feel discouraged, to cause you to be defeated, to make you doubt, and leave you in ruin so that destruction is your only option. The enemy uses this strategy because he knows that your victory is already secured. Actually you are **MORE THAN** a conqueror. Romans 8:37 says,

"Nay, in all these things we are more than conquerors through him that loved us."

When you learn how to recognize the strategies of the enemy in the moments of life, you can fight back relentlessly knowing that even his best attempts have already failed!

There is a story in the Bible about a man named David. I encourage you to read it for yourself. It begins in 1 Samuel 30. David settles in a city called Ziklag as he is on the run from a king named Saul who threatened to kill him. The Philistines were preparing to fight King Saul, so David along with some of the men from his city went to be an ally of the Philistines in the battle. Upon their arrival, the Philistines decided they did not want their assistance (probably because David was known for decapitating Goliath, one of the Philistines' champion fighters) and they requested that David and his men go back to their home in Ziklag. What David and the men found when they returned home was devastating. It should have been a celebration because none of the men had lost their lives in the battle; instead, there was mass chaos and havoc. The Amalekites had invaded the city while they were gone taking their wives, burning the city, and taking their children too.

Now, it is one thing when the enemy messes with your stuff but when he messes with your help, your home, or your hope, a different type of fight should rise up within you. There is symbolism in the city being burned and the women and children being removed from their home. The women represented their help, Ziklag was their home, and the children represented their hope for the future. You have to understand that when the enemy is out to master you, he comes for those things in your life that will leave you ineffective, uncovered, and hopeless. As a result of the complete loss looking them squarely in the face, David and the men that accompanied him lifted up their voices and wept until they had no more strength to weep. Sometimes you will face places in your life where you will cry until your tears run out of water—that's a moment!

For David, conditions quickly progress from bad to worse because the men that were once ready to fight alongside him had now turned against him and were conspiring to stone him. David had every right to be offended. He could have surrendered to the pressure of all that he was facing. He could have believed the voice of his circumstance and viewed himself as a victim of vicious events beyond his control with giving up as his only option. Instead, David encouraged himself *in the Lord his God.* David took a moment to go to the Master and that moment changed his outlook. That moment positioned him to receive a word of encouragement that would give him the strength and resiliency needed to fight again. That one moment with the Master reaffirmed his role as a leader and he once again led the men that were plotting to kill him to victory and recovery of that which was lost.

David was not isolated in his moment, just like you and I are not isolated in our moments. I am sure Joseph had a moment when he was thrown into a pit by his own brothers (see Genesis 37:23-24). The children of Israel began to have a moment when all they could see was the Red Sea in front of them and the threat of Pharaoh and his army behind them (Exodus 14:9-13). The widow woman had a moment when the creditor was trying to take her two sons to be bondmen (2 Kings 4:1).

Naturally, when you come home after a long, tiring day at work trying to make ends meet, only to find an eviction notice on your door, it will cause you to have a moment. When your spouse cusses, fusses and raises hell at home and can only seem to find Jesus at church or around church folks, that will cause you to have a moment. When your past tries to hold you hostage with memories that seem to say that what you have done is too bad for you to move forward, it will cause you to have a moment. If you mishandle the moments in your life, chaos is inevitable.

Everyone that has a moment has an opportunity to make a decision. Even right now you have a choice to make because I am sure you have had or are facing a moment. Will you take your moment to the Master and find strength in His unfailing promises? Or, will you stay in the place of desolation because of how circumstances appear? Your moments will never master you when you learn how to take them to the Master. The temporary moments in your life will not cause you to default on the divine destiny that God has promised you, because you belong to the Master and He will teach you how to master every moment.

A Place Called Process

So often those that survive the *moments* of life become despondent in the place called process. Process is the place where you deal with how you feel so you can heal. I wish I could tell you that it is an easy place. I wish I could give you some simple steps and tell you that the pain will just vanish away, but honestly sometimes the only way out is through. Even when going through is your only option, it is your choice how you go through. You can grow through it or you can go through it. Either way, there is always something to be gleaned from whatever you are going through. Some of the most painful seasons in my life taught me the most valuable lessons and provided me with an opportunity to depend on God like never before.

Process is that in-between place that is uncomfortable. It is the place where the pain is not as painful but it still hurts. The place where what you see presently does not totally look like what God has promised. Process is the place between expectation and manifestation where your flesh will fool you into following your feelings instead of standing in faith. I often remind others going through the place called process that feelings are fickle! Feelings are often fleshy and fleshy is always messy! However, faith is real and your faith is what matters most in the place called process. Your faith in God and His promises will take you further than your feelings any day.

Often times in the place called process, you will have to *faith it* even when you do not feel it! I am sure the widow in 2 Kings Chapter 4 felt forsaken, abandoned, overwhelmed, and perhaps hopeless, but when the creditor threatened to take her sons she stepped out of her feelings and stood in faith. She stood in faith because the present threat was greater than the past pain. You must understand the spiritual principle hidden in her experience. The enemy is never after your history. He is always after your destiny. He is out to destroy everything you have been anointed to birth, build, or will be blessed with that brings God glory. His assignment is to steal, kill, and destroy (John 10:10) while The Father's desire is that you would have life and have it in abundance. When you begin to understand that it is God's desire to bless you, you will stop cursing the process even when it is painful. You will keep pressing in faith believing that all things are working together for your good as Romans 8:28 states,

"And we know that all things work together for good to them that love God, to them who are the called according to his purpose."

Process is not a pretty place but it is necessary. There were some lessons and seasons in my life that if I could have opted out of them, I would have done so. I am sure that you can relate. Some of the situations that we encounter are so distressing that we cannot see any sense in them nor make any sense of them, but as my daddy often says, "You just keep on living." Keep on living and perhaps you will see that your place called process will be used to strengthen you and encourage someone else. Calvary was part of the process for our Lord and Savior Jesus Christ. It was not a pretty place but it was necessary for our deliverance and restoration of our divine destiny. If we become lost in the cross alone, we will forfeit the power, life, and strength that are granted after weathering the process.

Becoming lost in the cross means being consumed by the agony of the cross or trials that we experience and never being strengthened enough to walk effectively in victory. Calvary was a part of the process for our Savior Jesus Christ, but after the crucifixion there was a resurrection. The cross that you are bearing is part of the process but the power that you will gain after enduring is going to be phenomenal.

Process will purge you and prune you, but most importantly, perfect you. To **purge** means t*o rid (someone) from an unwanted feeling, memory or condition; to make free of something unwanted.* As you transition through the place called process you must purge yourself of anything that will hinder you spiritually. Some people are encumbered with bad habits, unhealthy relationships, and painful memories that hinder progression towards emotional well-being and freedom. Naturally, some have a tendency to hold on to things that they intend to use but never actually follow through. This takes up space and creates clutter. Do a self-assessment right now. What is cluttering your life and taking up the space that is reserved for God? What bad habits, unhealthy relationships, and painful memories are you holding onto that you need to relinquish? What are you holding onto that you need to purge? Failure to purge during the process can and will cause you to be burdened and hindered from moving forward.

Pruning is defined as *cutting back or cutting off parts for better shape or more fruitful growth.* Pruning is the painful part of the process. Pruning requires a cut, a removal, and a separation in order for growth to occur. Pruning is like embracing tough love; loving yourself enough to disconnect from everything that will hinder you from being all God desires. In gardening, pruning cuts away the tip bud and when you remove the dominance of the tip then that which was dormant begins to grow vigorously. Listen, there are some habits, thoughts, ways of thinking, and behaviors in your life that have been dominant and ultimately have been stifling your growth in the Lord. I challenge you, as you are going through the process, to allow God to prune you so that your dormant gifts, talents, and abilities can spring forth like never before.

God promises in His word to perfect you. The word perfect is not indicative of you having no mistakes or flaws but rather you being whole – nothing missing, nothing broken nothing lacking.

1 Peter 5:10 states,

"But the God of all grace, who hath called us unto his eternal glory by Christ Jesus, after that ye have suffered a while, make you perfect, stablish, strengthen, settle you."

It is after the pruning and the purging that you are perfected.

In your life you will have crosses to bear. They will not be easy; in fact, they are often harrowing and almost unbearable at times. However, there is strength in the midst of your struggles. There is a grace for the place that you are in so that the process does not cause you to pause but rather to persevere. If you become lost in the moment, in the pain of the cross then you will never embrace the power that is available after enduring the process. The fact that you survived is an indication that you are stronger than you think. The truth is the worst of what you encountered could not destroy you because your destiny is greater than everything you have been through!

Yes, you may have suffered a loss and in a moment everything you knew to be normal may have changed. However, just as David went from tragedy to triumph and just as the widow found a reason to stand in faith when her feelings screamed quit, it is my prayer that you will be strengthened to transition. Even now allow faith to transition you so you are not limited by fickle feelings but launched into a place of victory. It is my prayer that the pain of the process and your past experiences will not render you helpless or hopeless, but rather that you will begin to look around and see that even in the midst of great catastrophe you were not shattered. It does not matter how bad it has been or how bad it is, you can begin again and build again. Press through the place called process knowing that the affliction is temporary but the strength received after you endure will permanently bless you.

Remove the Residue

Merriam Webster Dictionary defines **residue** as *a usually small amount of something that remains after a process has been completed or a thing has been removed.* Many people survive the place called process but fail to thrive beyond that place because they fail to remove the residue of the experience. Removing the residue requires you to lay aside the remnants of offense, hurt, and any other negative emotion that may weigh you down. Residue can limit your potential and hinder your ability to move forward. Removing the residue of past hurt is never easy. It requires you to use the power of choice. Will you be vindictive or victorious? One position requires that you put your life on hold, waiting to see someone pay for the residue you are currently encumbered with. The other allows you to release the residue knowing that God is just and He will ultimately allow it to work together for your good.

If you are not careful the residue of your past will poison your present state of living causing you to curse your future. In 1 Chronicles 4:9-10 a story is told about a man named Jabez. His mother named him Jabez because she bore him in pain. It is not known whether it was an economical hardship or a difficult labor that gave inspiration for the name of Jabez. However, we know that in a moment that should have been joyful she transferred the residue of her experience to her son that had never faced what she had been through. Jabez's mother permanently named him out of what she felt in a temporary moment. Had she known what she was carrying she would have never named him "pain." You have to be careful about naming situations in your life pain when they may be blessings in disguise.

Jabez went to God saying,

> *"Oh, that you would bless me indeed, and enlarge my territory, that Your hand would be with me, and that you would keep me from evil, that I may not cause pain!"*

In that short prayer, Jabez asked God to remove the residue and reverse the word curse placed upon him by someone else. Despite the residue that he was born into, Jabez went to the One that is able to change his name without changing the letters that made up his name. Scripture records that Jabez was more honorable than his brothers because he asked God for a blessing for which they spent time fighting. Jabez went to God and God granted his request. Please note that Jabez's mother's name is not recorded in scripture. Do not miss this – sometimes God will allow "no name" people to position you for God-ordained blessings. Stop wasting your pain or blame on "no name" people! No name people are those who are not relevant or are insignificant to your process. Stop giving them more attention in your life than they deserve. Do not allow the residue of your encounter with them to stop you from accessing the blessings you are entitled to receive. Rather, focus on what God wants to grant you because they cannot curse what God has blessed. Do not become so consumed in the pain of the labor that you forget to embrace the deliverance!

If you do not remove the residue you will constantly rehearse what they did or what they said or what they think. The more that you rehearse it, the more you go in reverse. It is time for you to move forward. The world needs to know how you were able to remove the residue of what you have been through. Let me caution you – removing the residue is not about pretending that you are over it but rather petitioning God to change the name of what you have been through from *pain to power*. You are asking God to transform your past hurts from *pain to power*. It is about being reminded that what God says about you is greater than what they have called or "prophe*lied*" over you. Slowly but surely you can remove the residue if you are committed to work through the pain.

Removing the residue involves one key word – move! Right now, take an assessment of your connections, even in your thought life. Determine if there are nouns – people, places, things or ideas – that that you need to let go of so you can move forward. If you need help in removing the residue in your life, join me in the following prayer:

Father, I thank You that You know the thoughts that You think towards me and Your plans are to prosper me. Father, remove the residue of everything in my life that is not pleasing to you. Remove unforgiveness, bitterness, guilt, shame, blame, and anything else that causes me to remain in the place of a victim when you have called me to be more than a conqueror. Forgive me for the times that I limited Your divine assistance because I made my pain bigger than Your promises concerning me. I ask now Father that you would remove the residue of past hurt, past pain, and past experiences that would keep me from becoming all that You desire. I bind up the spirits of guilt and shame as a result of poor choices that I made and I loose strength and peace as a replacement. I bind up any transference of spirits and I plead the precious blood of Jesus against the word curses and the opinions of others that do not line up with Your Word and Your will concerning me.

Father, I ask that You would remove the residue and disconnect me from any present associations that are destructive to me spiritually, emotionally, financially, mentally, and physically. I receive divine restoration according to Your will in every area of my life and I trust that even while the residue is being removed You are drawing me closer to You. Thank You Lord for being concerned about every detail of my life! Thank You for allowing all things to work together for my good and Your glory.

In the precious name of Jesus, Amen.

The Challenge of Change

Change will challenge you whether you are ready or not. Starting over can be exciting and uncomfortable at the same time. Living beyond what is familiar can be unsettling at times. Ultimately, it is up to you to decide whether change will serve as a catalyst for success or with a limited scope, view change as a setup for failure. Change requires that you make adjustments, alter your course or direction, embrace modifications, and sometimes allow for a total life makeover.

Not all change is bad. Change is actually necessary. Change challenges you to move out of your comfort zone, face reality, take responsibility, and be accountable for your actions and choices. As it relates to the pain of change, not all pain is bad either. When a woman is in labor, the pain of the contractions alert her that change has arrived and it is time to push. It is your choice whether you will remain in pain or push through it and embrace the challenge of change. You must recognize that there is untapped potential inside of you. You must begin to see that the situations you have experienced were not for your destruction but a divine escort to your destined place of victory.

I had a plant that appeared to be dying. The leaves were withering, turning a yellowish brown, and falling off. I was watering and nurturing the plant but nothing was helping. One of the many mothers that God has blessed me with since the passing of my mother assessed it and said, "It needs to be repotted." At that same time, I was going through some situations in my own life and was fighting a change that was necessary. Like the plant, I was withering spiritually and my strength and peace were falling off and becoming nonexistent. My plant had outgrown where it was and I had outgrown my excuses to remain in a place of pain and offense. We repotted my plant and it began to grow vigorously; it was vibrant and full of life. It was no longer dying a slow death in a place that was once safe but over time became a space that would suffocate its potential to grow.

My mama, without the plant's permission, flipped it upside down and pulled it out of the old pot. She did this confidently because she knew the temporary process of repotting would set the plant up to grow bigger and better than ever. Mama did not care about her hands getting dirty; she wanted the plant to survive and thrive. Honestly, in that season of my life, I could identify with how my Mama was treating my plant. I felt like God had flipped my world upside down. He was confident that the change would be for my good and ultimately for His glory, despite how I felt. God knew that what He had in store for me was bigger and better than the place where I had settled. He did not mind getting His hands dirty to pull me out of my messy small pot mentality.

God repotted me like that plant but in the spiritual sense. He changed the soil that I was rooted and grounded in. God allowed me to become rooted and grounded in His Word and not words of negativity or past hurts. As a result of being rooted and grounded in His Word, strength came and growth was inevitable. But it was not easy because I was used to a "small pot." Small pot thinking causes big problems because it limits your ability to move forward. I learned during that period of change that familiarity can be fatal. I was familiar with a place that was slowly suffocating my destiny when God had so much more in store for me. Guess what? God has so much more in store for you too. Just like my plant that began to grow vigorously and come to life again after being repotted, there are some gifts, talents, and abilities in you that cannot manifest until change challenges the greatness locked up in you!

The difference between us and my plant is that we have the power of choice. Even when God loves us enough to "repot" us without warning we still are allowed to decide how we will respond to the change. Perhaps you have been resisting change not realizing that you are crying and concerned about something that you have outgrown. You know, sometimes negatives are necessary. When I was young, I had a camera that required film in order to take pictures. Once you finished taking pictures after they were developed you received the negatives along with the standard sized images. The negatives were distorted but they were needed to produce the actual picture. Use your power of choice to focus more on the big picture and not be distracted by the negatives. The negatives in your life are necessary because they prepare you to produce something greater. Do not forget even in the midst of the negative experiences, God sees the big picture! No matter how distorted things appear to be right now God is working on the big picture in your life and He does all things well.

Return to Sender

Even after successfully surviving the challenge of change, life at times will still have dark seasons. In this hour, I believe that the enemy is after the endurance of the saints by using discouragement and deception. The enemy is using discouragement because he wants you to become weary in well doing so that you do not reap ALL that God has for you. Deception is a strategic attack he has launched in an attempt to make believers comfortable *next* to the will of God. However, being *next* to the will of God and being *in* the will of God are two completely different positions. For example, if I invite you to ride with me to the mall and you stand *next* to my car you are deceived if you believe you are going anywhere. When I drive off you will be left behind because you were standing next to my car and not in the car. Being next to my car would cause you to miss your ride to the appointed destination just like being next to the will of God can hinder you from walking in complete victory.

As a result, people are now looking for a convenient Christianity instead of a committed Christianity. Those who participate in a lifestyle of convenient Christianity reach for God when they feel it is beneficial. Convenient Christians act like they are doing God a favor when they give of their time, talent or their treasure while forgetting that everything belongs to Him. This type of Christian is unstable, lackadaisical, and often uses the phrase, "only God can judge me" as an excuse to remain in unrepentant sin. Those who participate in a lifestyle of committed Christianity understand that a relationship with God is not an option but a necessity. The committed Christian understands that is a lifestyle of self-denial. Mark 8:34-36 shares this:

> *"And when he had called the people unto him with his disciples also, he said unto them, Whosoever will come after me, let him deny himself, and take up his cross, and follow me. For whosoever will save his life shall lose it; but whosoever shall lose his life for my sake and the gospel's, the same shall save it. For what shall it profit a man, if he shall gain the whole world, and lose his own soul?"*

The Committed Christian understands that they are not perfect but constantly seeks the Lord that they may be perfected. Committed Christians will give of their time, talents and treasure without seeking recognition because their desire is that God be glorified. This type of Christian understands that though the afflictions of the righteous are many the Lord will deliver them out of them all (Psalm 34:19).

A spirit of deception is running rampant and producing spiritual babies that have no desire to grow up. These spiritual babies are looking to be held, pacified, pampered, carried, and never responsible for anything. This has happened because some leaders in the body of Christ are teaching – sometimes unaware – people to be consumed by a personality rather than being concerned with the will and Word of God. This deceived church has become full of powerless performers that know how to act churchy but have not mastered how to live holy. Sadly, they are now a people that cannot endure anything. It is the deceived church that has produced people that always want to be recognized, are often offended, always the victim, and constantly looking to be pampered and pacified.

In 2 Timothy 2:3-4, the Apostle Paul was encouraging Timothy, but I believe we can receive helpful encouragement from his letter as well. He states,

"Thou therefore endure hardness, as a good soldier of Jesus Christ. No man that warreth entangleth himself with the affairs of this life; that he may please him who hath chosen him to be a soldier."

You must know from this day forward that your Commander in Chief of your soul is also the CEO of the universe and He is consumed with ensuring that you succeed. You must maintain a proper perspective if you are going to be counted worthy of being called a good soldier. You have to be able to decipher the voice of your heavenly Father over the voice of the enemy. You must remember that the same One that brought you through with victory on the mountain top is the same One that will bring you through in the valley.

When you hear a voice that does not line up with the voice of God, you should immediately RETURN TO SENDER! The United States Postal Service has an option available when unsolicited merchandise arrives to your address. You can mark on an unopened package "Return to Sender" and the Postal Service will send it back at no charge to you (see Publication 300-A - U.S. Postal Inspection Service Guide to Preventing Mail Fraud June 2010 PSN 7610-04-000-6946 – Unsolicited Merchandise). Sometimes satan will send unsolicited merchandise to your spiritual address in the form of doubt, discouragement, or fear and you need to know that is your spiritual right not to receive it or entertain it but return it to the sender. For example, if the enemy sends discouragement and says, "You can't make it, you will never be successful, you should just give up…," you should not receive that but return it to the sender because it is a lie and it does not line up with the Word of God or the will of God concerning you. Returning it to the sender means that you take the lies of satan and replace it with what the Word says about your situation. In this example, the Word of God states that you can do all things through Christ because He's going to supply you with the strength to get it accomplished. The Amplified version of Philippians 4:13 says,

> *"I have strength for all things in Christ Who empowers me [I am ready for anything and equal to anything through Him Who infuses inner strength into me; I am self-sufficient in Christ's sufficiency]."*

This chapter will revolutionize your life if you allow it. You do not have to receive anything that does not confirm God's purpose and His divine will for your life. It does not matter if what you are hearing is your own thoughts, the words of someone really close to you, the opinions of someone else, or perhaps the thoughts of a man or woman of God. If it does not line up with the word, return it to the sender. You have to be careful about who you listen to because the same way we use vehicles to arrive to point B from point A, the enemy uses people to accomplish his desires in the earth. If you are not careful you will allow a lie from the enemy to talk you out of your destiny.

This almost happened with Elijah. First Kings 19:1-3 says,

> *"And Ahab told Jezebel all that Elijah had done, and withal how he had slain all the prophets with the sword. Then Jezebel sent a messenger unto Elijah, saying, So let the gods do to me, and more also, if I make not thy life as the life of one of them by to morrow about this time. And when he saw that, he*

arose, and went for his life, and came to Beersheba, which belongeth to Judah, and left his servant there."

In order to understand the significance of what is taking place you should pause for a moment and read 1 Kings Chapter 18. Elijah had just returned from a major God assignment and victory on the mountaintop. One threat from the enemy hurled him in a downward spiral that led to a failed suicide attempt. There are a couple of points that stand out in this passage of scripture. The first is that Jezebel sent a messenger to tell Elijah that she was going to kill him. Instead of sending a messenger, she could have sent the hit man himself – the person that would have been assigned to kill him. But she did not have the authority to take Elijah's life because he was under divine protection by God. Just like Elijah, you have to know in faith that you are divinely protected by God.

Secondly, it says when he **saw** what she said he ran for his life. The enemy was strategic. He used Jezebel to say something that would move Elijah off course and out of position. Then after threatening to kill him, Elijah became so discouraged that he ran away into the wilderness and asked to die. If you are not careful, the enemy will set you up for major defeat after some of your greatest victories. And if you believe the voice of the messenger he sends your way, you will be planning to quit your defeat while God is working on your destiny and your next assignment.

You have to know how to return to sender when it does not come from God. The spirit of Jezebel comes to silence the voice of the prophetic. Pastor Ronald Thornhill did a teaching on the spirit of Jezebel. He shared that Jezebel is not a woman in scandalous clothing with lots of makeup and red lipstick as was the opinion of the traditional church. Pastor Thornhill shared that the spirit of Jezebel operates through three separate strategies and those are manipulation, intimidation, and domination. Upon further study, I have discovered what he shared to be very true. Just as Jezebel used her words to intimidate Elijah and manipulate him into fear so she could dominate and seek to carry out her ultimate desire which was to destroy him, so it is with some leaders in the body of Christ. Some leaders in the body of operate under the spirit of Jezebel, using their office to intimidate people by manipulating them with impure motives and ultimately dominating them to the place where people begin to fear them more than they do God. GOD IS NOT PLEASED! God promised to give us pastors according to His heart but leaders with the spirit of Jezebel have perverted that promise. Jeremiah 3:15 states,

"I will give you pastors according to mine heart, which shall feed you with knowledge and understanding."

In God's heart there is no manipulation, intimidation or domination. The spirit of Jezebel is harmful to the believer. It seeks to silence the voice of the prophetic and disrupt every promise that God has made concerning you. You must know for yourself that God plans to prosper you and the spirit of Jezebel cannot stop God's plan for your life. Moreover, Jeremiah 29:11 says,

"For I know the thoughts that I think toward you, saith the LORD, thoughts of peace, and not of evil, to give you an expected end."

God has a divine expectation for your life that will bring peace and not evil. So whenever God has made a promise to you the spirit of Jezebel will attempt to intimidate, manipulate, and ultimately dominate you with a spirit of fear so you forfeit the peace and the prosperity that God has promised you. This is why it is so necessary that you ask God for wisdom, discernment, and most importantly study and learn the Word of God for yourself. When you know the Word of God you will be able to identify the voice of God because whatever God says will not contradict His Word. You need to know the voice of God for yourself and you have to know when it is time for a divine override. A divine override places you in a position where you hear God's voice over everything and seek His will no matter what distractions the enemy throws your way.

Be careful about what you see. Check the address on the package and if it is not coming from God or does not line up with the Word of God – return to sender! Sometimes the enemy will try to send you temptations, distractions, and discouragement. Perhaps he will even try to send guilt and shame because of past mistakes and failures. Regardless, none of those things are edifying to you spiritually and you need to return those opportunities and temptations back to the sender. God has changed your address because 2 Corinthians 5:17 states,

> *"Therefore if any man be in Christ, he is a new creature: old things are passed away; behold, all things are become new."*

You are a new creation in Christ Jesus with a new spiritual identity and address. So when the enemy tries to send you pacifiers or other things that would please your flesh and hinder your spirit, maintain your position in God. When you begin to maintain your position in God the address will be *undeliverable*, God will fight your battles for you and return all foolishness back to the sender.

Pack Up the Pity Party

There is no power in self pity. Self pity involves a negative focus and a pessimistic perspective. Pity of one's self because of mistakes or failures can be an open invitation to discouragement or depression. Pity can poison your perspective because you can become so lost in the limitations of what you see that you begin to pack away your potential and attempt to place God in a box. Sometimes you will make decisions that seemed good initially but as time progresses you may realize it was not the best choice. Spending time dwelling in a place of regret will only cause you to waste more time and miss out on valuable opportunities. Learn how to move forward without regrets.

Moving forward without regrets can be difficult because some people enjoy having a pity party. Actually, some have a subconscious list of people that they attempt to invite to pity them as well. I believe the devil is the event planner for pity parties and anything he plans ends with destruction. Do not allow the devil to cause you to stay in reverse and continually relive the pain of an experience that God has already released you from. The first step in moving forward is removing your right to be pitiful. Often times, people throw pity parties when they believe they are the only person that has ever experienced what they are facing.

News flash – YOU ARE NOT THE ONLY ONE WHO HAS…

- Failed a test
- Lost a job
- Lost a spouse
- Been cheated on
- Been lied too
- Been fired from your job
- Had a failed relationship
- Felt overwhelmed
- Struggled to make ends meet
- Been a single parent
- Never been married
- Been tired
- Lost a home
- Lost a child
- Been through a breakdown
- Been through a divorce
- Been through an illness

The list could go on but you understand the point. You are not the only one that has ever been through whatever it is that you are currently facing.

Secondly, most people that host pity parties say that no one understands and that is a lie. People that host pity parties often do not desire to be understood, they seek an audience to validate what they FEEL is their right to remain in pain. I tell my friends sometimes, "If you look to be offended you will always find a reason." Believing no one understands sets you up to isolate your devastating experience as unidentifiable and as a result, irreconcilable. Even when you do not understand your situation, God sees, God knows, God cares, and He is always there.

Thirdly, people that host pity parties are backwards and nearsighted spiritually. Please do not be offended but hear me out so I can help you out if it applies to you. Everything about you was created to go forward. In order to see all that is behind you, eventually you will have to turn your body along with your neck. If you try to keep walking forward while you are looking behind, at some point you will end up tripping, walking into something, or hurting yourself. Spiritually many of us have at some time in life tried to move forward while looking at our past and as a result we ended up tripping, walking into a trap, or hurting ourselves.

Going backwards when everything about you was created to go forward will cause you to be in bondage. God was so concerned about your future that He paid the price so your forever would be spent with Him. So why would you subject yourself to misery and being filled with regret by looking at past mistakes and failures when you are supposed to be enjoying the journey to eternity? Isaiah 43:18-19 (NKJV) encourages us to forget former things:

"Do not remember the former things, Nor consider the things of old. Behold, I will do a new thing, Now it shall spring forth; Shall you not know it? I will even make a road in the wilderness And rivers in the desert.

In context, through this portion of scripture God's people had been down, bound, and in captivity for so long that

God sent a word to encourage them (just as He has sent this book to encourage you).

God identifies Himself as their Redeemer. He assures them that He will deliver them from their oppressors and the place of their oppression. God speaks and encourages them to forget the former things because He is going to do a new thing. He states He will make a road in a place that is rough and rocky and He will place a river in a place that is supposed to be dry. But in order to see what He was going to do they had to let go of the bondage they had encountered. They could not afford to have a backwards focus because God was preparing to bring them forward.

I wear corrective lenses because I am nearsighted, meaning that I can see objects that are close, but in order to see objects that are far away I need visual assistance. When you become so consumed by the situation you are in that you cannot see God nor see your way out, you need spiritual visual assistance. The Word of God is what serves as corrective lenses providing visual assistance to those that are discouraged or overwhelmed. Sometimes life will make you nearsighted. Life will cause you to be consumed by what you see immediately. However, through spiritual visual assistance with the Word of God you will not be overwhelmed but instead positioned to be an overcomer.

God is taking you forward! Not backward and not to a place nearby but He has a divine destination for you that is far away from the pain and devastation that you have endured. Let me encourage you – your history is not bad enough to stop your divine destiny.

If you remain in self pity, you will rehearse all that has been done and ultimately remain in reverse, stuck and unable to move forward in a healthy manner. Yes, your pain is real. Yes, the hurt was real, but God is real too and He is greater than any hurt or pain that you will ever face. You have to be willing to exchange your pity for His power. You can be pitiful or powerful – the choice is yours.

Pass Me a Pillow

"On the same day, when evening had come, He said to them, "Let us cross over to the other side." Now when they had left the multitude, they took Him along in the boat as He was. And other little boats were also with Him. And a great windstorm arose, and the waves beat into the boat, so that it was already filling. But He was in the stern, asleep on a pillow. And they awoke Him and said to Him, "Teacher, do You not care that we are perishing?" Then He arose and rebuked the wind, and said to the sea, "Peace, be still!" And the wind ceased and there was a great calm."
Mark 4:35-39 NKJV

I've learned that peace is not the absence of troubles; peace is not the absence of problems; peace is not the absence of persecution; but peace is the presence of your faith in an all present, all powerful, all perceiving God. Holding onto your faith in the midst of a storm is not always easy. Storms, naturally, hide the sun and oftentimes the storms of life will hide the Son. The storms of life are not prejudice. The storms of life do not care how well you have planned or how much you have prayed. There is no exemption; at some point, a storm will visit you. Actually, even while you are holding this book I would be wise to suggest that you are in one of three stages. You are either coming out of a storm, in the midst of a storm, or preparing to go through a storm.

Some storms are life storms – common trouble that comes with everyday life. But then there are some storms that we bring on ourselves. You have to be careful of the choices you make, remembering that there are always consequences. Also, be careful of stormy people. Stormy people are unstable and unsettled. They change like the wind and are quick to rain on your parade. They have the tendency to state, "If I was you, I would do…" but rarely are they doing anything but complaining and remaining. They always have a problem, a complaint, or are mixed up in drama of some type. Stay away from stormy people when possible and bask in the "Sonshine."

In the beginning of this chapter I shared a passage of scripture. In summary, Jesus stated to His disciples, "Let us cross over to the other side." They got in the boat and headed across the water. What Jesus did not tell them was that they would encounter a storm. Also, He gets a pillow and goes to sleep. Out of seemingly nowhere, a storm arises and the disciples begin to question the Master's concern for their very lives stating, "Teacher, do you not care that we are perishing?"

Have you ever been there? Did you hear clearly from God about your next step and prepared for smooth sailing only to encounter a storm and feel like He had gone to sleep on the job? Have you ever prayed and felt like Heaven was silent and what you could see was so threatening that it caused you to question what God said? Maybe that is not you and congratulations on your excellent faith, but for those of you who have faced some difficult situations and do not mind taking off your mask for a moment, allow me to encourage you. This storm allowed them to meet Jesus in a totally different capacity. They met the One that was able to control the winds and the waves. Sometimes the storms in our lives are an opportunity for the Master to introduce Himself in a manner by which we may have not known him before.

Jesus rose and with three simple words – Peace, be still – He rebuked chaos and restored order. In that moment, those that had been walking with Him consistently were afforded an opportunity to know Him more powerfully. Storms give us a greater revelation of who God is and a greater revelation of the Word that has been spoken.

Let us glean this revelation from the disciples' experience. Jesus said, "Let us *cross over* to the other side." (emphasis added). God cannot lie so when the Word speaks a word it is surely coming to pass. The disciples received the word that they were going to the other side. However, Jesus did not tell them that they would encounter a storm during their journey and feel like they were stuck in the middle of a raging sea. He only allowed them to know they were going to the other side. If the disciples had a total understanding of who was on the boat with them they would have grabbed a pillow as well. Jesus was able to sleep because of what He had already stated. You should learn how to rest on what He said. The whole premise of pass me a pillow is learning to get in the Word of God even when storms are raging and being able to rest on what God said in the midst of the storm. You do not have to stay up at night anymore, you do not have to pace the floor consumed with worry anymore – get a pillow and rest in His Word. When people try to bring you drama, instruct them to pass you a pillow. When you learn how to stand on the Word of God you will learn how to rest when the wind blows and sleep during storms. Allow the Word to carry you across life's stormy waters!

• • •   49   • • •

Get Your Faith Up

There is a debilitating disease that has become a worldwide epidemic. This disease cripples the confident, stifles the strong, and destroys the determined. It is a five letter word that has caused graveyards to be filled with should've, could've, and would've. It is a five letter word that keeps dreams from being fulfilled and stops visions from materializing. That five letter word is doubt.

To doubt means to be

- uncertain about;
- to consider questionable or
- to consider unlikely;
- to hesitate to believe;
- to distrust;
- to fear or be apprehensive about

Doubt is the antithesis of faith. Actually, the absence of faith is the presence of doubt. Faith is essential to the spiritual life of any believer. When you want to know whether or not God is pleased all you have to do is take an assessment of your faith. Hebrews 11:6 states,

"But without faith it is impossible to please him: for he that cometh to God must believe that he is, and that he is a rewarder of them that diligently seek him."

Faith is like a muscle. In order to be strengthened, it has to be stretched. I love how faith is defined in Hebrews 11:1 of the amplified version of the Bible:

> *"Now faith is the assurance (the confirmation, the title deed) of the things [we] hope for, being the proof of things [we] do not see and the conviction of their reality [faith perceiving as real fact what is not revealed to the senses]."*

Did you see that? It said now faith is the assurance, the confirmation, the title deed. When you have the title deed to something you do not have to make payments for it because you already own it. Faith causes you to be able to have access to whatever you need and you will not have to pay for it because God is willing to grant it to you!

Faith is easy when everything is going well but the question is can you still trust God when your life is a living hell. It is the enemy's desire to see you faint, grow weary, and give up. He wants you to experience a syncope which is defined as a loss of consciousness usually experienced after a drop in blood pressure. When someone faints they become unaware of their surroundings. The enemy wants you to lose spiritual consciousness and forget that God has you surrounded. He wants you to forget that God has gone before you, stands beside you, and is behind you in the midst of everything that you go through.

When someone faints they are unconscious, they have no knowledge of what is going on. As a believer, when you faint you forget about how God made a way when you were struggling; how He healed you when you were sick; how He delivered you when you were bound. You forget that God was faithful in the last valley and He is well able to bring you through this valley. When you faint you allow your flesh to talk you out of what faith knows to be true. After all God has done for you, after all He has brought you through, and after all the times He made a way, it would be foolish to faint now. It would be crazy of you to listen to the devil (who by the way is already defeated) and allow him to talk you out of your divine victory. If the enemy is in your ear or providing suggestions in your thought life then he is out of order because he is supposed to be under your feet!

> *"Behold, I give unto you power to tread on serpents and scorpions, and over all the power of the enemy: and nothing shall by any means hurt you."*
> Luke 10:19 KJV

Faith is not about how you feel; faith is all about your expectation to see what God said concerning you. You have to know undoubtedly that God cannot lie – if He promised it, it shall come to pass. It does not matter how bad it looks or how long it takes. If God said it you can bank on it! The same ability to create based upon the spoken word is housed inside of you because of your divine DNA. Every time God spoke (see Genesis chapter 1) something manifested and every time you speak something will happen whether it is positive or negative. God did not waste His words and you have to be careful not to waste your words.

Regardless of how much power you have inherited spiritually by being a child of God, if you are not careful your feelings will fool the faith out of you. I believe such was the case with Peter. Matthew chapter 14:22-33 shares the well known story of how Peter walked on water. Peter exercised faith when he stepped out of the boat and began to walk on water. However, as he became distracted by the winds and the waves – what he saw – he became afraid and began to sink. His flesh began to see naturally the tempestuous environment, he began to fear, and his feelings fooled the faith out of him.

But it is good to know that even in times where our feelings get the best of us God loves us so much that He is willing to come to our rescue. Just as Peter cried, "Lord, save me." when he found himself sinking, we are able to do the same. Even when we start sinking in the very areas that we have power, authority, and dominion to walk successfully through, IMMEDIATELY God is there to rescue us and prevent us from being swallowed by the stormy currents of life. You must know that even when your faith wavers the Father's love for you is constant, consistent, and unconditional!

The Father looks upon you with compassion even when your faith has been fooled by your natural senses. As with Peter, He asks you "Oh thou of little faith, wherefore didst thou doubt?" Can you imagine what would have happen if Peter had BIG faith? Can you visualize the vast blessings God has for your life through the eyes of faith? God can and will change your whole life if you only believe.

F.A.I.T.H. = Forsaking All I Trust Him

Faith requires you to forsake your feelings, your thoughts and your opinions, and believe God relentlessly! Faith requires a total surrender of fear, doubt, and distrust. As you surrender in faith you will be strengthened in spirit. Faith positions you to believe God when the doctor's report is bad, when the odds are against you, and when bills are behind. Faith knows there is nothing too hard for God. When you have faith you will not be moved by the mountains you are facing but rather speak to those mountains and tell them to move! The application of faith is the difference between victory and defeat. Why? Because faith does not have to see victory to believe victory: rather faith believes victory so it always sees victory. What you believe you will see. Sometimes it may be immediately and other times gradually, but if you believe it you will see it.

When was the last time you truly exercised your faith and believed God for something that was beyond your ability to grasp or do? You may be in a faith exercise right now; allow me to encourage you. Faith is the resting place for miracles. If you can believe it, God is able to do it. Big faith brings about big miracles. TAKE THE LIMITS OFF OF GOD! Stretch your faith into the realm of the impossible because with God all things are possible!

Devastated But Not Destroyed

In May 2011 I ministered a sermon entitled "Devastated But Not Destroyed" at a conference in Hurt, Virginia. A snippet of that sermon is on YouTube under the same title. The overall message was about having resiliency in the face of adversity. I shared how the widow in 2 Kings 4:1 found herself in a devastating situation.

> *"Now there cried a certain woman of the wives of the sons of the prophets unto Elisha, saying, Thy servant my husband is dead; and thou knowest that thy servant did fear the LORD: and the creditor is come to take unto him my two sons to be bondmen."*

This certain woman who is not named found herself in a precarious position. As a result, desperation was birthed inside of her and a relentless tenacity to rise to the challenges she faced. Her response to her situation gives us a formula that is foolproof.

When devastation happens it births desperation.

Desperation + Determination = Deliverance!

Desperate times call for desperate measures. When devastation happens it will birth some sort of desperation. A desperation that will cause you to fight, flee or freeze. For this woman, her desperation birthed a fight in her because the creditor was coming to collect something that she could not afford to lose.

We can gather from the scripture that her husband's death was unexpected because he was with the sons of the prophets under the leading of Elisha. So we know that he was a man of God given to service, yet his death left his family uncovered and unprepared to settle a debt that occurred prior to his sudden departure. This certain woman could have had a pity party or become consumed by the challenges she faced but instead she went to where she knew she would hear God's voice. She was devastated. The departure of her husband represented her history but her sons represented her destiny and she had to make a decision at the crossroads of her crisis.

We all have to make a decision at the crossroads of our crisis. Do we become consumed by the crisis and allow our faith to become contaminated with our present pain. Or, do we choose to press through the devastation with a desperation that is undeniable by God. The woman went to the man of God and he asked her what she had in her house. All she had was a pot of oil. After receiving specific instructions the woman obeyed. I am sure she encountered looks, stares, whispers, and rejection, but her determination was relentless. Her determination was birthed out of a desperation that came as a result of devastation.

She had an assignment to go and collect as many vessels as she could from her neighbors. It does not say in the text that she went and announced to the neighborhood why she needed the vessels; she simply obeyed the instructions she was given. Once she collected the vessels, she was instructed to shut the door behind her and her sons. Next she was to pour the only thing she had left which was a pot of oil into the vessels she collected. What happens next is miraculous.

> *"And it came to pass, when the vessels were full, that she said unto her son, Bring me yet a vessel. And he said unto her, There is not a vessel more. And the oil stayed. Then she came and told the man of God. And he said, Go, sell the oil, and pay thy debt, and live thou and thy children of the rest."*
> 2 Kings 4:6-7

After selling the oil she had more than enough to sustain her family and prevent the creditors from coming to take her sons. This certain woman's blessings took place behind closed doors. She found deliverance because she obeyed and used what she had along with what she had gathered.

God is releasing blessings to you right now because you took the time to read this book. There are some "behind closed doors" blessings that He is making available for you right now. There is no doubt that the devastation was painful but you were not destroyed! If you are still struggling with devastation, allow it to give birth to a desperation that will birth a determination in you that will ultimately birth your deliverance.

Let's pray.

Lord, I believe that Your plans for my life are good. I believe that you plan to prosper me. I acknowledge that at some point in my life I have faced devastation. Help me to properly package the pain of my past so that it does not hinder me as I move forward. Right now God, I will to let go of offense, bitterness, and any hurt that I have harbored as a result of devastation. I ask now that my desperation for will birth a determination in me to desire that Your will be done in my life. As a result, I thank you in advance for the deliverance that I am receiving even now.

Lord, I thank You that You are going to teach me how to master the moment even when life happens. Thank You that after the place called process you will remove the residue and help me embrace the challenge of change. As I move forward God, give me the wisdom not to waste my time with pity parties but rather to allow Your Word to become my pillow so I can rest in Your promises and know that even when I face devastating situations I will not be destroyed.

In Jesus' name, Amen!

To contact the author for speaking engagements, conferences, book tours and book signings in your church or organization, write or call:

Pastor Jessica L. Jones

Phone:
(434) 878-0987

Website:
www.devastatedbutnotdestroyed.com

Email:
abndntlyblssd1@icloud.com

Follow her Blog:
www.getyourfaithup.com

About Pastor Jessica L. Jones

A fixture of inspiration, motivation, hope, and new life, Pastor Jessica L. Jones encourages, exhorts, and empowers all to reach their full potential in their personal and spiritual lives. Chosen by God, anointed for His purpose, and on a divine assignment to win souls to the glory of God, Pastor Jessica has been called to push men and women from labor into delivery so that the divine assignment on their life is both birthed and fulfilled.

Fueled by a passion to see people live up to their full potential and walk in the greatness God destined for them, she merges spirituality with the practicality of everyday life. Pastor Jessica's approach provokes everyone to pursue and live a life of integrity and holiness. She believes in training up warriors who will allow their faith to propel them even when they may not see the fullness of what God is doing in their lives.

Pastor Jessica allowed the Lord to fulfill the divine purpose of her existence in February 2005 when she was licensed into ministry. God saw fit to elevate her assignment and as a result she was ordained as an Evangelist in July of 2009. Most recently, in January 2011 she was appointed to the office of Youth Pastor. As a result of her faithfulness to the mantle on her life, God has allowed her ministry to span the East Coast and beyond. Pastor Jessica is anointed by God to preach the gospel with a prolific, profound and prophetic word that will set captives free! However, her greatest desire is that God be glorified through her life!

She is the daughter of Mr. and Mrs. Sherman Jones, Sr. and has been singing in The Lord's House since the age of three. She is a graduate of Brunswick County Public Schools and Longwood University in Farmville, VA, where she obtained a Bachelor of Science Degree in Social Work.

Other Authors by

DMI PUBLISHING HOUSE

We speak of spiritual warfare in the same mindset as physical warfare. We have approached it with thoughts of violent and vehement confrontations. In actuality, spiritual warfare is best fought using simple biblical principles. 100 out of 100 people are offended, the offender, or both. This book is intended to teach one of the most basic, yet most powerful principles - and that is the principle of forgiveness.

ISBN: 978-0-692-30523-2

For more information, visit
www.forgivenessisaweapon.com